It's Sunday afternoon. Dad says,
"Let's go for a drive!"

My sister groans. "That is so boring."

She thinks everything is boring.

I like Sunday drives. I sit in the back,
behind Mom. From there, I can watch
Dad driving.

Someday I'll be in the driver's seat!

I smile and wave at everyone we pass.

Mom tells Dad to slow down.

I fog up the window and write a message.

Bowser does too.

Sometimes I fall asleep in the car.

I never know where we'll be when
I wake up!

Maybe Dad will drive us to the beach.

Maybe he'll take us to Grandma's house.

Maybe we'll go to the zoo!

Today Dad drives us to nowhere special.

I think this is the best drive of all!